Hope to Hop

by Paige Patterson
illustrated by John Whitman

Practice Decodable 19

McGraw Hill Education

Bothell, WA • Chicago, IL • Columbus, OH • New York, NY

MHEonline.com

Send all inquiries to:
McGraw-Hill Education
8787 Orion Place
Columbus, OH 43240

ISBN: 978-0-02-144969-9
MHID: 0-02-144969-4

Printed in China.

8 9 10 11 12 DSS 27 26 25 24 23

Jan likes to flip.

She makes a plan.

Go get ten big men to help.

Five at a time, men get set.

Eve jumps.
Eve sends Jan up.

Jan hopes to hop on top.
Did she get there?

Yes!

Jan got up there.

Practice Decodable 19

Hope to Hop

High-Frequency Word Reviewed in Practice Decodable 19

there

Previously Reviewed High-Frequency Words

a
all
am
and
as
at
be
boy
but
can
did
do
down
for
girl
go
had
has
have
he
her
him
his
I
in
is
it
little
look
of
on
out
said
see
she
that
the
they
to
up
was
we
were
what
with
you

Sound-Spelling Correspondences in Decodables

1. /s/, /m/, /d/, /p/, /a/
2. /h/, /t/
3. /n/, /l/
4. /i/
5. /b/, /k/ spelled *c*
6. /o/, /r/
7. /g/
8. /j/, /f/
9. /u/, /ks/ spelled *x*
10. /z/
11. /w/, /k/ spelled *k*
12. /e/, /kw/ spelled *qu*
13. /y/, /v/
14. Long *a* spelled *a_e*
15. Long *i* spelled *i_e*
16. Long *o* spelled *o_e*
17. Long *u* spelled *u_e*
18. Long *e* spelled *e_e*
19. Review

SRA Open Court Reading

Practice Decodables

Grade K
Practice Decodable 19
Hope to Hop

MHEonline.com

978-0-02-144969-9
MHID 0-02-144969-4

EAN
9 780021 449699
99701

McGraw Hill Education

Grab

by Jacob Blakeslee
illustrated by Chris Vallo

McGraw Hill Education

THIS BOOK IS THE PROPERTY OF:

STATE ______ PROVINCE ______ COUNTY ______ PARISH ______ SCHOOL DISTRICT ______ OTHER ______	Book No. ______ Enter information in spaces to the left as instructed

ISSUED TO	Year Used	CONDITION	
		ISSUED	RETURNED

PUPILS to whom this textbook is issued must not write on any page or mark any part of it in any way, consumable textbooks excepted.

1. Teachers should see that the pupil's name is clearly written in ink in the spaces above in every book issued.
2. The following terms should be used in recording the condition of the book: New; Good; Fair; Poor; Bad.